Seymour Simon

BRIDGES

SeaStar Books • San Francisco

To Jeremy and Chloe

Permission to use the following photographs is gratefully
acknowledged:
Front cover, pages 18-19: © Peter B. Kaplan/Photo Researchers; title page:
© Andy Levin/Photo Researchers; pages 2–3 © Art Gingert/Comstock;
pages 4–5: © Rafael Macia/Photo Researchers; pages 6–7: © Peter
Groenendyk/Photo Researchers; pages 8–9, 30–31: © David
Frazier/Photo Researchers; pages 10–11: © Eitan Simanor/Bruce
Coleman Inc.; pages 12–13: © Richard Hamilton Smith/Dembinsky
Photo Associates; pages 14–15: © Comstock; pages 16–17: © CORBIS;
pages 20–21: © Bettmann/CORBIS; pages 22–23: © Joseph Sohm/Photo
Researchers; pages 24–25 : © Lowell Georgia/Photo Researchers; pages
26–27: © David Davis/Photo Researchers; pages 28–29: © Toshitaka
Morita/PPS/Photo Researchers; page 32: © John and Barbara
Gerlach/Visuals Unlimited; back cover: © Comstock

Thanks also to Bruce Stephan, PE,
for his expert reading of this manuscript.

Book design by E. Friedman.
Typeset in 18-point ITC Century Book.
Manufactured in China.

SeaStar is an imprint of Chronicle Books LLC.

Library of Congress Cataloging-in-Publication Data
Simon, Seymour.
Bridges / Seymour Simon.
p. cm. — (Seemore readers)
ISBN 1-58717-264-X (Paperback); 1-58717-263-1 (Library Edition)
1. Bridges—Juvenile literature. 2. Bridges—Design and
construction—Juvenile literature. I. Title.
TG148.S48 2005
624.2—dc22
2004024579

Distributed in Canada by Raincoast Books
9050 Shaughnessy Street, Vancouver, British Columbia V6P 6E5

10 9 8 7 6 5 4 3 2 1

Chronicle Books LLC
85 Second Street, San Francisco, California 94105

www.chroniclekids.com

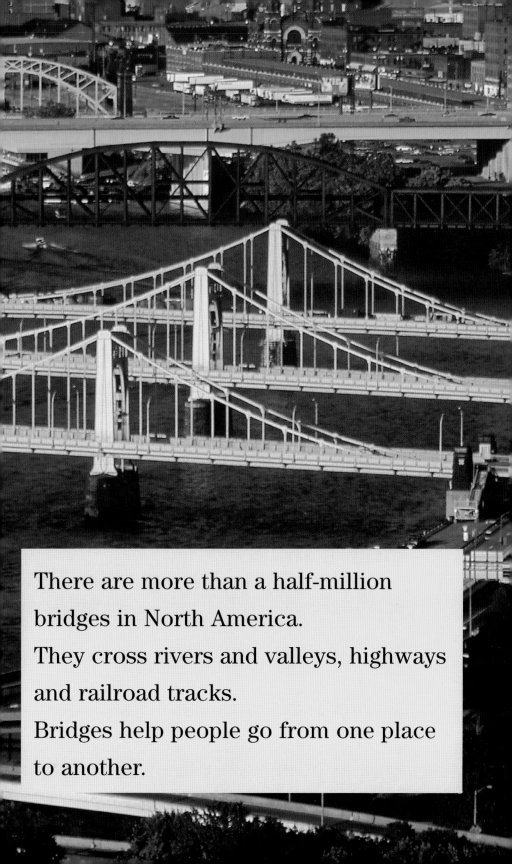

There are more than a half-million
bridges in North America.
They cross rivers and valleys, highways
and railroad tracks.
Bridges help people go from one place
to another.

The Ponte Vecchio (PON-tee VEK-io) in Florence, Italy, was built more than 600 years ago.

It replaced a wooden bridge built by the Romans hundreds of years earlier. It is still in use, and today tourist shops line both sides.

The Tower Bridge was built more than a hundred years ago over the river Thames in London.
The middle of the bridge rises to permit large ships to pass beneath.

There are three main kinds of bridges: beam, arch, and suspension.
Engineers decide which kind of bridge is best for each place.

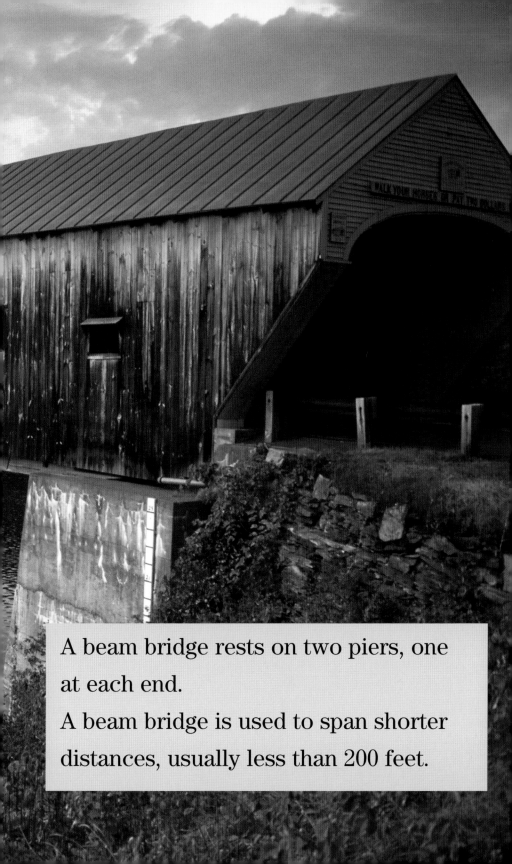

A beam bridge rests on two piers, one at each end.

A beam bridge is used to span shorter distances, usually less than 200 feet.

The Firth of Forth Bridge, near Edinburgh, Scotland, is a truss bridge, 1½ miles long. A truss bridge is a kind of beam bridge that uses steel triangles to help support the bridge.

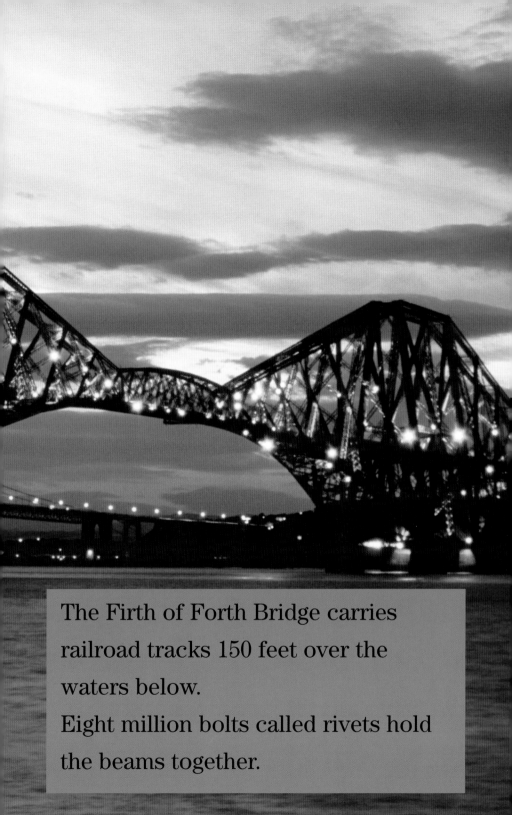

The Firth of Forth Bridge carries railroad tracks 150 feet over the waters below.
Eight million bolts called rivets hold the beams together.

An arch bridge is a semicircle with a pier at each end.
The weight of the bridge pushes along the curve of the arch toward the piers.

Two thousand years ago, the Romans built stone and brick arch aqueducts that carried water.
Modern arch bridges are made with concrete and steel.

Suspension bridges can span the longest distances.
When the Brooklyn Bridge was built across New York City's East River in 1883, it was the longest bridge in the world.
One hundred and fifty thousand people paid one cent each to walk across the bridge on opening day.

Heavy steel cables strung between towers hold up the roadway of a suspension bridge.

The towers are built hundreds of feet high at both ends of the bridge.

The cables loop over the towers and are fastened into strong anchors in the ground.

Wire ropes called
suspenders hang
down from the cables
and attach to large
steel beams.
A strong roadway
is laid on top of
the beams.

When it opened, the Tacoma Narrows
Bridge was called "Galloping Gertie"
because of the way it swayed in the wind.
Drivers said that crossing the bridge
was like riding a roller coaster.
On the morning of November 7, 1940,
the bridge began to twist and shake
in 40-mile-per-hour winds.
Suddenly, it broke apart and fell.
This disaster changed the way
suspension bridges were designed.
Rather than blocking the wind, new
bridges allow the wind to blow
through them.

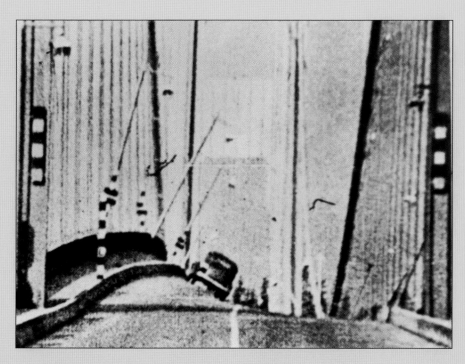

The Golden Gate Bridge, near San
Francisco, was built to withstand
high winds, ocean waves, and even an
earthquake.
One of its piers sits in the open water,
100 feet below the surface.

Below the pier is a block of concrete bigger than a football field.

If you laid the steel wires used to make the cables in this bridge end to end, they would be long enough to circle the world three times.

A long roadway of bridges and tunnels stretches over Chesapeake Bay for nearly 18 miles.

The roadway follows two high suspension bridges, several truss bridges, many low beam bridges, and two mile-long tunnels. These bridges have more than 5,000 piers. The bridge-tunnel dips over and under the open waters of the bay.

Each year, millions of cars drive along the bridges and seem to disappear from view as they enter the tunnels, which go under the water.

The Sunshine Skyway in Florida is more than 5 miles long and soars 190 feet above the waters of Tampa Bay.

Twenty-one steel cables painted bright yellow support the roadway. Six large concrete islands, called dolphins, were built in the bay to support the piers.

Each dolphin can withstand a crash from an 87,000-ton ship.

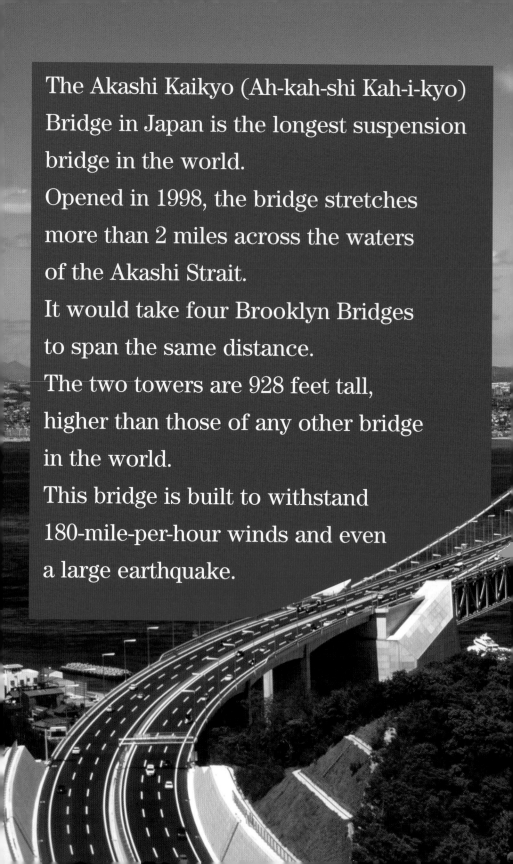

The Akashi Kaikyo (Ah-kah-shi Kah-i-kyo)
Bridge in Japan is the longest suspension
bridge in the world.
Opened in 1998, the bridge stretches
more than 2 miles across the waters
of the Akashi Strait.
It would take four Brooklyn Bridges
to span the same distance.
The two towers are 928 feet tall,
higher than those of any other bridge
in the world.
This bridge is built to withstand
180-mile-per-hour winds and even
a large earthquake.

Many bridges in North America are more than fifty years old and will have to be replaced.

Bridge engineers use computers to help design modern bridges.

The Alamillo (ala-ME-yo) Bridge, in Seville, Spain, has a single upward column supporting the entire weight of the roadway.

In the future, bridges will span longer distances, support heavier loads, and be less expensive to build.
No one knows how far these new bridges will be able to reach.